Retire
On
Purpose

RETIRE ON PURPOSE
A Financial Blueprint to Protect Your Family and Preserve Your Wealth

ISBN: 978-1-956220-30-8

www.ExpertPress.net

Expert Press
2 Shepard Hills Court
Little Rock, AR 72223
www.ExpertPress.net

Editing by Tamma Ford
Copyediting by Lori Price
Proofreading by Abby Kendall
Text design and composition by Emily Fritz
Cover design by Casey Fritz

Retire
On
Purpose

A Financial Blueprint to *Protect* Your Family and *Preserve* Your Wealth

Alynn Godfroy
The Financial Architect for Canadians™

Contents

Opening Comments

It was in 2017 that I published my first book, *Why You Need A Financial Advisor.*[1]

A lot of things have changed since then, including my becoming a mom in 2017 and our world experiencing a global pandemic. My husband also recently retired at the age of fifty, which has been a big change in our household.

My first book talked about why, at different ages, people would be wise to have a financial advisor.

For example, in your twenties, having an advisor to give you the various options you have to pay for your first house or a range of strategies to pay off student loans is of vital interest to you. More and

---

1   *Why You Need A Financial Advisor*, Alynn Godfroy: *https://www.amazon. com/Why-You-Need-Financial-Advisor-ebook/dp/B084DSQ3GJ.*

more twentysomethings are seeking out expert guidance—today's youth are just savvier than we were at that age. Doing this kind of planning prevents too much of your money from being gobbled up right at the start of your working life; it can give you perhaps more disposable income for the rest of your life.

But let's just fast forward to your seventies. You'll need expert support working on an estate plan, making sure you have the proper wills and powers of attorney in place, a strategy for elder health care, or options for leaving a legacy to kids, grandkids, and charities.

> *You don't even think of such things in your twenties, do you?*

So, why this book?

I thought it was important to now do a book more specifically for the age group that I enjoy working with the most and whom I think would most benefit from my expertise. These are people between the ages of fifty and seventy who are planning for retirement or just entering retirement. If the number "seventy" seems old to you, we are not our grandparents' generation! We live healthier for more years and therefore often choose to work longer.

In my profession, the process of saving for retirement is called "accumulation," and we should be doing it from our very first paycheck. The act of spending that money during retirement is called "decumulation." This should not be done haphazardly, but according to a clear organization of your money and a careful strategy for spending it. Why? So you don't run out of money while you are retired.

If you are in this fifty to seventy age group, you will find you need to know how to properly decumulate your assets and properly structure any legacy you wish to leave for your kids and grandkids. In addition, you'll want to make sure you have enough money to live on so you can be comfortable for the rest of your life.

I have chunked down the information you might need to *R.E.T.I.R.E.* in the following way:

Review Your Foundation

Envision Your Future

Trim Your Taxes

Insulate Your Income

Reinforce Your Wealth

Establish Your Legacy

One of the things I would like to stress before you really dive into reading this book is that the examples and stories of people in this book come from real life. The stories are 100 percent true. However, you know the old saying: I have changed the names (and a few of the details) to protect the innocent! I will always ensure the privacy of my clients, have no doubt.

I have lived most of my life in Windsor, Ontario, which is a very blue-collar town where many of my clients are auto workers, health-care workers, civil servants, and trade workers. The average household income of my clients is probably somewhere between $150,000 and $180,000. This is not to say I don't have clients making less than that or households making more than that. This is just the range for a dual-income household I most often see in the clients I work with. Most clients also have at least $300,000 of investment assets by the time I meet with them.

When you're reading this book I want you to realize the stories I'm telling you are about average everyday people. In their stories you can learn how people have done very well with their money. You can also read how things people did could have been improved upon with the guidance of a financial advisor who is well-versed in organizing your finances and in tax planning.

One thing I'd like you to keep in mind: It is not so much about the amount of money you earn or believe you need to have saved before you retire, but more about planning wisely for the money you have. It is clear that Canada's tax structure is daunting, so you won't have all the answers you probably need by cruising the internet. You probably won't understand the intricacies of the pension you have been saving into for decades. Come and see me with all your questions. My team and I will be able to give you (usually comforting!) answers and if needed, help you reorganize your finances for your best retirement.

Chapter 1

Review Your Foundation

You know that your retirement is not going to be all about money. But for a comfortable retirement that lets you have and do all those "non-money" things, you really do need to look at what I will be calling your financial foundation.

For most people who work, there will be multiple sources of income and they unite to create your *financial foundation* in retirement.

You probably already know what they are, but let's itemize them for clarity, starting with the obvious sources of money you have.

Personal Assets and Income

While all of your money is "personal," I have divided what you voluntarily do with your money from what you do because you are in a system (pensions and so on). Starting with the obvious, you earn wages or a salary. You have personal cash savings.

From your cash savings, you have perhaps put some in a personally managed trading account; perhaps you earn dividends from some of your stock investments.

You might earn royalties from a published book or recurring sales of an invention.

You also might have a multilevel marketing business, run a digital business, do some type of consulting work, or have another type of "side gig" using your tradesman skills that brings in money, even as you continue to work full-time elsewhere.

Many of my clients own real assets such as primary residences or vacation homes without monetizing them. But others of you might invest your earnings over time into income-producing real estate rental properties, Airbnb units, or income-producing land.

You might have invested in a partial or absentee business partnership. Business ownership may take not just the brick-and-mortar but also the digital form that we call an online business.

Perhaps you own a cottage or another major asset and plan on selling it when the value has significantly risen; you think you will set aside the after-tax profit for your retirement needs.

These are all potential sources of personally generated income you have that can extend into your retirement. These are typically part-time sources of income.

I often caution my older clients about launching so-called "income-generating activities" right at retirement. I also discourage hanging on to such opportunities that are not producing income after a few months or which don't show a consistent profit. Why? No, I'm not a killjoy. I have simply seen more than once how they might cost you more of your retirement income than you think and create an income loss for you instead of an income gain. If you are younger and have three to five years to develop such an income source, it will allow you to keep earning salary or wages elsewhere as you grow the new income source for yourself into a long-term money stream or a predictable residual income.

Less common as an income source, you might have had a cash or asset windfall through an inheritance or trust fund and not spent the money. Like the profits from the sale of a major asset (real estate or other), you should consider placing this cash in a safe haven, an interest-producing instrument. Talk to me about some of these. I can help.

Lastly, take a look at the types of insurance you carry, such as tax-sheltered life insurance policies. Some policies may serve as mortgage and income protection. Some might have a cash surrender value you can use to add to your retirement income.

> **This is the big picture for your personally, voluntarily generated income.**

Wisely structuring that income after retirement is our main subject in these pages, but let's look first at how Canada's government-managed programs work to provide you with income after retirement.

Canadian Retirement Benefits: CPP and OAS

There are two main government-administered retirement programs: CPP, the Canada Pension Plan, and OAS, Old Age Security.

Those of you who have worked are eligible for the CPP. It is useful to know how CPP, the Canada Pension Plan, is funded.

Throughout your working life, your employer contributes 5.7 percent to your plan and you contribute 5.7 percent as a paycheck withholding. If you have been self-employed, you know you have been paying 11.4 percent or the whole amount, since you are seen as both employer and employee (this amount has progressively increased over the past few years as it used to be 4.95 percent for the employee and 4.95 percent for the employer for quite some time).

How do you find out how much you are eligible for? While the earliest eligibility is age sixty, you'll be earning 30 percent less by taking it then than if you wait until the more typical age of sixty-five.

For those of you who have been residents in Canada long enough, OAS (Old Age Security) is another source of retirement income. On average, most people will get OAS of about $642 per month (but see one common exception in a later chapter). Call "Service Canada" to ask how you stand for that benefit.[2]

Canadian Pensions: DCPP, DBPP, and RPP

There are three main employer-administered pension plans. While most people have only one of these

---

2   https://www.canada.ca/en/contact/contact-1-800-o-canada.html.
     Telephone: 1-800-O-Canada (1-800-622-6232); **TTY:** 1-800-926-9105;
     From outside Canada: Call 1-800 O-Canada from abroad.

plans, some of you might have more than one due to a diverse career.

1. DCPP, the Defined Contribution Pension Plan
2. DBPP, the Defined Benefit Pension Plan
3. RPP, the Registered Pension Plan

Each of these plans differs in how you can later withdraw the funds. The differences revolve around taxes, limits to your withdrawal amounts, and your obligation to withdraw. Each plan is also different in how the employer matching works.

Voluntary Personal Cash Savings: RRSP, TFSA, and Non-Registered

In addition to the earlier ways I listed for people who voluntarily save, many of you have probably saved into registered accounts or other tax-free instruments.

These are plans you can voluntarily save into (i.e., not employer-administered). Withdrawing money without penalties from each one comes with rules that you can ask me about. These plans are:

1. RRSP, the Registered Retirement Savings Plan or a Group RRSP (these are similar to the USA's 401(k) plans with company match)

2. NRSP or NRA, the Non-Registered Account (such as a stock market trading or mutual fund account)

3. TFSA, the Individual Tax-Free Savings Account

There are tax advantages to many, if not all, of the plans I have named when you manage them properly and as designed. On an income of $70,000, for example, the Canadian tax rate is 29.65 percent. By saving into the RRSP (and other such plans), you reduce your tax bill through a refund to your tax filing.

The government allows you to grow your RRSPs tax-deferred until you are seventy-one years of age, then your RRSPs must be turned into RRIFs— Registered Retirement Income Funds. From age seventy-one, a 5.28 percent withdrawal is the minimum and it is progressive to about age ninety-two at that rate and represents $5,281 per year.

TFSA: Optimizing Your Tax-Free Savings Accounts

I truly believe the Tax-Free Savings Account, the TFSA (the third plan on my list above), is the most underutilized financial investment available to Canadians now.[3]

3   https://www.canada.ca/en/revenue-agency/services/tax/individuals/
topics/tax-free-savings-account/contributions.html; https://www.cana-
da.ca/en/revenue-agency/programs/about-canada-revenue-agency-cra/
income-statistics-gst-hst-statistics/tax-free-savings-account-statistics/
tax-free-savings-account-statistics-2019-tax-year.html

A TFSA is integral to any Canadian's financial foundation—or should be. In 2009, the government announced that any Canadian aged eighteen or over could put $5,000 into this account. The beauty of a Tax-Free Savings Account is that you don't pay tax on any growth the account earns. When you withdraw the money, you likewise don't pay tax.

The only tax paid on this account was when you earned the employment income or other income on the cash you initially put into it. That, to me, is a big, amazing *wow*!

The benefit of the Tax-Free Savings Account is greater than a one-time $5,000. Back in 2009 when the government allowed you to put $5,000 into the account, they also allowed Canadians to make the $5,000 deposit every single year.

Here is a list of all the back years and how much you can contribute toward each of those years:

YEAR	CONTRIBUTION AMOUNT
2009	$5,000
2010	$5,000
2011	$5,000
2012	$5,000
2013	$5,500
2014	$5,500

YEAR	CONTRIBUTION AMOUNT
2015	$10,000
2016	$5,500
2017	$5,500
2018	$5,500
2019	$6,000
2020	$6,000
2021	$6,000
2022	$6,000
2023	$6,500
Total	$88,000

How could this look for you? Say it is 2011. You didn't put money in the TFSA in 2009 or 2010. Now in 2011, you would be allowed to deposit $15,000 in your TFSA. You could do this because for those three specific years you have $15,000 of "contribution room."

Now fast-forward to the publishing date of this book, which is 2023. If you have never opened a Tax-Free Savings Account and were eighteen years of age or older in the year 2009, then you would be able to contribute $88,000 right away. If you're married (a spouse or common-law partner) and your spouse/partner also had never opened a TFSA, then your spouse would also have that same $88,000 contribution room in the TFSA account.

Again, this is one of the most underutilized accounts available to Canadians. Come in and talk to me about setting it up!

Unfortunately, when the government gives something, you need to be mindful that sometimes there is a catch. With the TFSA, if you over-contribute, you could end up being penalized.

Tracking Your Contribution Room

As I said, our nation's tax structures are complex, and if you get it wrong, you risk paying penalties. This is also the case with the TFSA if you are not attentive.

If you put too much money into the TFSA in a given year, the government will penalize you if you don't remedy the situation promptly. The government will charge you 1 percent of the over-contributed amount *per month*. If you don't catch your over-contribution early on, the penalty amount can add up very quickly.

It's fairly easy to avoid any such penalties if you just pay attention to how much you put into the account over the year(s).

REAL PEOPLE: **Know Your Eligibility!**

A couple, Kristof and Ramona, came in to consult. They were not born in Canada but had worked throughout their years here. They thought they could retire about now, and Ramona wanted to know, "What do you think, Miss Alynn? Can we do it?"

They were eligible for only about half the typical OAS amount due to their twenty-four-year residency in the country. It is important to know that Old Age Security differs from the Canada Pension Plan as OAS is simply based on residency whereas CPP is paid based on contributions you make as a percentage of your working income. The benefit is calculated on your years of Canadian residency after age eighteen.

Kristof was already taking CPP, though he should not have been, and wanted to retire by age sixty-two. We looked at their numbers together. They owned an income-producing rental property, so I noted that amount. They had a son on disability who got a $900 per month stipend for those expenses; however, it wasn't enough to fully cover the costs his care incurred. We looked at their reduced OAS.

They were a hiccup away from a derailed retirement, financially speaking.

Additionally, they had spread their money with three or four advisors. This lack of consolidation meant that none of the advisors was giving sound, fully informed advice; I also noted they were not getting great returns on the money placed with the various advisors.

They needed a plan. I crunched their numbers and showed them they needed to work for another year or two before retiring. Kristof and Ramona were still young enough to do so and did it willingly. I also suggested they gently raise the rent on their rental property, consolidate their investments with one advisor, and look at instruments that earned a higher return (they were actually in funds that were a little too conservative for them based on their risk tolerance). Knowing how much they will have in retirement in two years gives them no small amount of comfort.

REAL PEOPLE: Include All Your Income Sources!

A single mom, Crystal, came to me. She was in her midforties. Due to a conversation with another financial advisor, she believed she would need $3 million to retire. She was in a panic. "How can I possibly save that much on what I am earning?"

Crystal was in tears with fear. She didn't believe she could ever accumulate that much of a nest egg by retirement. She was afraid of retiring in poverty. She was losing sleep over this financial concern.

Her former advisor probably spit out that number after running a 3 percent payout to get to a $90,000 per year income. I believe he did this because Crystal was in the health care profession and earning about that much per year in salary.

I played detective to determine her total financial foundation by asking her lots of questions. As I asked and she saw that she did have resources, she perked up more and more.

As it happened, the other advisor did not take into account her CPP, OAS, or RRSP amounts. He didn't even factor in this monthly income that she would qualify for in her retirement years.

I told Crystal her CPP and OAS would generate around $2,000 a month. We added her RRSP.

The other advisor had also not questioned her about any passive income or other investments she might have. It turned out she had a rental property already generating a net of $1,800 per month for her.

When I added all of her sources of income and showed her what her retirement funds would be (as calculated in her forties, of course), she was all smiles. Crystal already had more for her retirement than she imagined.

Then I asked her about her current expenses. How much did it cost her every month to run her household? She figured she was spending about $4,500 per month right now. Even when I calculated potential future inflation and did some simple math for her, she would only need to save around $500,000 above and beyond the CPP, OAS, RRSP, rental income amounts, and her tax credits. She also had nearly twenty more years to save that amount, and I demonstrated how much to save per year. When she realized saving that sum was totally feasible on her income, she nearly fainted with relief.

I showed, literally by the numbers, that there was no way she had a gap of $3 million for her retirement expenses.

This was a no-obligation meeting with her. She was so relieved to know she didn't need to sweat and slave to put aside $3 million in savings that she moved all of her money to our company to manage. We discussed ways to invest that new cash savings of hers so it would grow—and thus help generate the amount she needed to make up the difference. No more sleepless nights for her!

REAL PEOPLE: **TFSA Contribution Room**

Cindy is a client for whom I track the TFSA contribution room. I am her authorized tax preparer, so I can actually monitor the information on the government website for her.

However, Cindy did not realize an error she was making. When she went to the credit union where she does her day-to-day banking, she was putting money into what she thought was her traditional savings account. It turned out that she was mixed up. She was putting the money into her TFSA.

Unfortunately, I didn't know about this additional savings account she had, or I would have caught it for her in time. As it happened, Cindy got a nasty letter from the government stating that she had over-contributed $10,000 that year. Well, $10,000 at a 1 percent penalty per month is $100 per month—a $1,200 penalty.

Correcting things simply requires immediate action on your part. What the government typically does first is send you an "Educational Letter." Basically, it is warning you that you have over-contributed to your TFSA. This is your notice to withdraw the excess amount right away. As long as you get the letter and withdraw the funds in a timely fashion (the letter will tell you how long you have to do this), you are penalty-free. However, if you fail to correct things or commit a second infraction in a later year, they are not so nice. They will require you to pay the 1 percent penalty.

Chapter 2

Envision Your Future

Many of my meetings with clients might sound like a heart-to-heart talk to someone listening in. And often they are! I am very willing to talk with you about your needs in retirement.

I find that some clients have deeply considered their finances and their goals for retirement. But when I discover that you have no plan, I move into action. I book a meeting with you to do what I call clarity-based planning.

Clarity-Based Planning

You have retired. Financially, all your basic needs are covered. Many of you have a bit of extra money during retirement and can spend some of it on things you wish to do—but what is it exactly you wish to spend it on?

You now have an extra forty to sixty waking hours a week on your hands. What do you see yourself doing with them? How do you wish to be spending your time?

Time and money. It allows you to consider activities, hobbies, and goals for your retirement years. Let's call it your wish list.

For some, a new "work" or "business" activity is on their wish list. They can work it part-time and still feel like they have their hand in the game, so to speak. They'll say it keeps them alert and involved in the world.

For others of you, it might be about a dream of living in Florida or Costa Rica as a snowbird for four months every winter in your own condo that you rent out as an Airbnb for the rest of the year. Can you see treating yourself and a younger grandchild or two to an annual world cruise or one month every summer touring Peru or Italy?

What would you like to be doing with your copious free time in retirement? That helps you (and me, as your financial advisor) clarify your financial requirements. So, while picturing your life as a retiree, let's circle back to the money you will need.

Basic Needs in Retirement

Covering your core needs in retirement is far and away the first consideration in any financial planning. No doubt, it needs to start with a roof over your head and being able to eat daily. Needs may also include access to complete medical services and care, a safe and reliable means of transportation, and an adequate wardrobe for our climate. But isn't that about it? The rest are wants. They are things we wish to have or desire but could easily live without.

To have a clear idea of how much money you will have not only for those needs but how much is leftover for your wants, I always recommend writing up a Cash Flow Plan. (I have put this three-page form in the Resources and References section at the end of this book.)

This is a combination of budgeting today's expenses and needs and doing some thinking to make sure your future needs are covered. In the process, you see the amount of available cash you have left to pursue some items on your wish list.

A Cash Flow Plan will illustrate two things that I find most of my clients are not considering. It shows you:

- which of today's expenses you might still have in retirement along with which expenses will go away, and

- how much income you have coming in during retirement after tax is paid.

An example of the first expenses that will roll over from today into your retirement is your costs for housing and food. However, these might be different from the costs you had raising a family. By your retirement, your kids are likely no longer "on your payroll" but out on their own—presumably out of school, earning their own income, and living in their own place.

That means that as retirees you can downsize your lodgings. Living in smaller places might mean a lower utility bill and maintenance costs. Kids grown and gone also means you might not be feeding as many family members every day. Retired means you no longer have commuting costs and probably do not need a costly work wardrobe anymore.

It is my second point that is revealing to most people. When people don't calculate how much after-tax income they'll have in retirement, they often believe they cannot yet afford to retire. Most working people are so stuck on how much money is withheld or taken out of their gross paycheck, that they imagine this will continue into retirement. Not so.

Most people just don't know how their tax picture will change when they retire or what that does to their available income. This is why they fear not having enough money to retire. I'll dive into detail in the next chapter, but it will become part of your Cash Flow Plan.

Retirement Wish List

When you have written up all of your costs of living (the needs you will have to pay for), it is time to go back to your wish list for your retirement years. In other words, what are the wants, desires, activities, and goals that the money you've been accumulating will allow you to satisfy? Add it all to your Cash Flow Plan.

By drawing up a needs/wants budget—a cash flow plan—you can see how your financial needs change at retirement. Compare how much you spend on various line items while working against what the amount becomes upon retirement.

How does that look? Will you be driving less and saving on bridge or tunnel tolls and gas? Will you be spending less on clothing now that you no longer have to dress a certain way for work? Will you be downsizing your residence—selling your primary residence in favor of a smaller, less costly one—now that the children are on their own?

I watch my clients' expressions as they realize how their costs of living will change during retirement— and often in their favor! This is also when they realize they really do have extra money to devote to their wish list goals. The money they used to spend on commuting, work clothes, and eating out during a workday is no longer required. It can be allocated to their wish list. Grocery and utility bills in the big family house are lower now, and the unspent money can also go to the wish list.

Inflation: What You Need to Know

Inflation is a reality. In a nutshell, it means less purchasing power. One of your dollars buys less than before; we are seeing it in our post-COVID economy.

If you are on a fixed monthly income, inflation affects you. Everyday items and services are more expensive.

Beware of the banker or the investment advisor who talks with you only about market risk but never about inflation risk. Inflation is new for many professionals—we have not experienced much of it in the past ten to twelve years, so professionals have not been schooling themselves about the ramifications of it on fixed incomes during an inflationary period.

While none of us has a crystal ball, it is possible to simply assume inflation will eat away at some of your fixed income over your retirement years and take action to mitigate those effects. Make sure you are in the proper investments to lessen the effect of inflation by choosing instruments paying a bit more interest. I can give you some options.

Also, remember that we are living longer than our ancestors. Plan on living beyond a century—simply because you just might. You never know. In North America, there are tens of thousands of centenarians. Will you be one? Just imagining it usually wakes up my clients to the need to do this longer-term planning around money!

Health Care Costs

One important planning aspect for our elder years is a topic people often quite studiously avoid thinking about: deteriorating health.

My clients usually start our meetings by just asking about their income status throughout retirement. I'm often the one to bring up health issues and a financial plan to cover them.

What will happen to your health as you age? Like inflation during the remainder of our lifetime, we just don't know.

Please do not be squeamish about how your health and your health care needs may evolve as you age.

Think about your current or family health history. Think about the number of individuals you may already know who have required long-term care, nursing home, or assisted living facility support.

All of that costs money that you can plan for. Talk to me about it. I'll ask you the questions you need to think about. I'll give you the options you need to know about.

REAL PEOPLE: Money for as Long as You Live

A ninety-two-year-old woman, Elaine, came to me. Her banker had never had an inflation discussion with her. Her investments at the bank were earning 0.66 percent. Two-thirds of one percent! Definitely not enough, no matter how many millions of dollars a person might have (and she did not). Not in an environment of between 15 and 50 percent inflation of some of her basic costs! Elaine's advisors did not even propose moving her into a high-interest savings account.

Certainly, the low returns on her investments were negatively affecting her cash flow story. Recent high inflation had just made it worse.

Elaine is a perfect example of how we are simply living longer than our grandparents and ancestors.

If your retirement advisor is only running numbers to take you through age ninety (like hers was), and you live until age ninety-eight, (and she may just live longer than that), you will run out of money before you run out of life. Your last eight years won't be so great, financially speaking.

You'll have to run the numbers to age one hundred. I can do that with you. Keep in mind not only your family genetics and historical longevity but also your chances of living longer than any ancestors simply because of modern medicine, hygiene, and available health care.

REAL PEOPLE: The Impact of a Health Crisis

I've known my clients Jonathan and Suzette for many years. They had fully paid off their house and had over a million dollars in their nest egg by a fairly young age. Jonathan was the funniest storyteller and the most enjoyable person to be with. I have fond memories of New Year's Eve with him, Suzette, and other friends.

John was sixty-one or sixty-two when he began to experience a health issue none of us would wish on anyone we love: Alzheimer's. He could no longer formulate an understandable sentence. He couldn't make a sandwich for himself. This put Suzette into an unexpected caregiver situation. She will arrive at a point where she knows she cannot care for him 24/7 anymore, and Jonathan will need to go to a long-term health care facility.

This type of health deterioration can put a monkey wrench in your retirement cash flow plan. Think about chronic or lifelong illnesses, such as Alzheimer's or lingering cancer. Private nursing care homes start at about $4,000 per month and are more often at the $6,000 per month price point. What happens to your nest egg with that new cost eating away at it? While public homes are affordable, will that suit your needs?

A health issue is most dreaded in your elder years simply because you have stopped earning money. At a younger age, you could certainly go back out and earn new money to pay the bills such events left you with. But in retirement, it could derail your cash flow plan beyond recognition.

This is the very reason you should have a health care solution within your retirement cash flow plan as soon as you can implement it.

REAL PEOPLE: How Much is That Side Hustle Costing You?

I spoke to a lady, Rachel, this past year who is still working in a full-time salaried position. She put in some of her own money to start a side business offering counseling, for which she charged $140 per hour.

Rachel thought the side business looked promising, revenue-wise. Knowing she had only been a salaried employee up to that point, I asked if she was setting aside about one-third of her gross counseling earnings for tax. She had not thought about that! At tax time, she would have been in for a rude awakening if she had not put any money aside for the tax levy. As a salary earner, the withholdings had been done automatically. I also told Rachel to keep careful records of her counseling-related expenses, which would be tax deductions.

I gave her a couple of easy ways to track her money. She was thankful I mentioned it to her so soon in her business as a counselor.

I suggest you also consult a professional like me about the tax picture you might be facing with a side gig or a retirement business.

Another client of mine, Marissa, had four side hustles and wasn't making money at any of them. When her retirement comes along, she'll perhaps still be forking out hundreds a month to keep them afloat. Why? I cannot make decisions for my clients, only give advice. I hope Marissa lets go of those money losers.

Ask yourself if you are cut out for the work involved in a new business activity—and if you can do it profitably.

> **Don't lose your retirement nest egg by doing some business activity you would never have risked at age thirty or forty!**

Some people are encouraged by all the new free time they will possess in retirement to do an income-producing hobby or side gig, and that is fine. Just make sure it's not jeopardizing your tax picture, your total income, or your government benefits.

REAL PEOPLE: Understand Cash Flow and Budgeting

A married couple, James and Louise, consulted me. Both were eligible for a pension. They couldn't seem to get ahead financially. They never seemed to have enough disposable income to set aside as savings. Frankly, they were somewhat baffled as to why not. They both earned substantial incomes.

To their credit, they kept a written budget, so I helped them examine their budget, one line item at a time. We were basically embarking on some detective work. We analyzed the budget numbers one by one in relation to their bank statements. Like so many of us, nearly 100 percent of the spending James and Louise did was by a debit or credit card, so it was a straightforward exercise.

According to the budget sheet they kept, they were spending $200 per month eating out, which for them included restaurants, drive-throughs, to-go coffee every midday, and takeout or delivery in the evenings. All that was along with their regular grocery shopping for home-cooked meals.

By examining this budget line item in relation to their banking statements, they saw the eating-out budget was up to as much as $1,500 per month! James was shocked. Louise was baffled. Even though their additional grocery budget was right in line with what they had stated, their lack of disposable cash income for saving was all about them eating out . . . and spending loads more than either imagined.

Look at your out-of-pocket expenses. Debit and credit cards are the way we spend these days so you need a way to keep track of your expenses. Remember, merchants are starting to charge you up to 2.4 percent more, which is presumably a portion of the bank fee they must pay for card processing. More and more, tips are expected to be greater than 15 percent of your bill—and paying only 15 percent is often considered rude!

There was good news for this case. These clients were younger and could make a new lifestyle choice. They could start saving to catch up dramatically in their retirement cash flow plan. We had quite a long chat in my office about what kind of changes that would entail. I was sure the conversation would continue when they got back home and for days and weeks to come. Why do I say that? I know from personal experience that changing any long-term habits takes real effort!

REAL PEOPLE: Are You Ready to Retire?

I had a married couple, Frank and Terri, come in. They thought they wanted to retire in a couple of years and wanted to talk about retirement funding and get some of their questions answered.

Their combined disposable income—the excess cash they had after paying all their bills and taxes every month—came to $4,500 per month. Many people would like to be in that situation, right?

So why did Frank and Terri want to work for another couple of years? I asked them just that question.

To demonstrate to them how ridiculous it would be for them to continue working for another two years, I wrote "$200" on two separate sticky notes. I passed one over the table to Frank and the other to Terri. I dramatized a bit: "Put this on your dashboards, and when wintertime hits us hard and you're out there at 6:15 in the morning, in the cold, windy darkness, scraping the ice off your windshield to get to work— look at this sticky note. It will remind you that you're out there in the freezing weather at the crack of dawn for a mere $200 more a month."

That's all they would have gained by continuing to work. Frank said something unprintable; Terri got a big smile on her face. They got it.

If it is not clear to you, their income when working was only $200 more than their total retirement income would be if they retired immediately. Said in yet another way, why go to work for $5,000 per month when you can immediately retire with $4,800 per month?

Like most people, neither Frank nor Terri knew how to do this calculation (which is why I am in business), so I did a mock tax return for them. After taxes, union dues, and other expenses taken off a salary, they are left earning only $200 more per month than they would have if they were retired.

Why earn only $200 per month by continuing to work? I find myself asking many clients this question. I urged them both to retire at their earliest eligible age.

Chapter 3
Trim Your Taxes

Paying tax comes with earning money. We all get that. Entering retirement is a matter of understanding how much money you can retire with and a lot has to do with your tax picture. As I said earlier, many people are so stuck on how much is withheld from their paycheck for taxes or pension and the like while they are working, that they don't realize how this will change during retirement.

It is a much rosier picture than most people imagine, so let me paint the picture for you.

In Canada, the big picture about taxes starts with "credits" and a calculation called the "basic amount" of earnings.

The "basic amount" for everyone of any age in 2023 is $15,000 in gross annual earnings before a penny of tax is owed.

There is also a calculation called the "age credit." If you are sixty-five or older, the "age amount" kicks in and you can add $8,396 to the basic amount of $15,000. In other words, at that age, you can earn $23,396 per year before any tax is owed.

Now we come to "credits."

Pension Splitting

If you have a pension, you can get an annual $2,000 "pension credit." This is where most people miss the boat. If one of you is working and the other is retired, you can do "pension splitting." You share $2,000 with your spouse once a year, every year, and get a credit on your own tax forms—even if your spouse is still working. It's essentially a wash on taxes due.

Another type of credit is available to you if you put money from your cheque into a retirement plan that acts as a deduction during your working years. The pre-tax money you put into the plan grows tax-deferred, while your salary is taxed at a lower rate since the gross salary is reduced by your contribution. You will pay tax on the money in the plan as you withdraw it, with the assumption that when you retire and withdraw, you will be in a lower tax bracket. This is a great incentive to participate in these programs.

In case you are curious, when you get Canada Pension Plan and Old Age Security benefits, the dollar amounts typically fall under the basic amount I mentioned so there usually isn't any tax payable on the first $23,396 you receive. However, if you have other pensions and income, they will have to be added to your taxable income and will likely result in taxes payable.

Related to Pension Splitting

If you are leaving an employer, you might consider a severance payment spread—dividing the severance amount over two years. It might be about timing (if you resign in May, you won't want to wait for the whole amount until the following January) or other aspects of your tax picture. Come and ask me!

CPP Credit Sharing

What a lot of Canadians don't know is they can also apply to split money coming to them for the CPP, the Canada Pension Plan.

John worked forty years, making him eligible for the maximum CPP benefit of $1,200 per month. His wife, Mary, stayed home all those years and now is eligible for $400 in her own right. This brings the couple's CPP to $1,600 monthly.

Now, John can apply to assign credits to Mary and vice versa. John assigns $800 of his CPP to Mary, and Mary assigns $800 to him, creating an even split of the $1,600 between them. This is called CPP credit sharing.

Taxable income is reduced due to this splitting of credits. This is only eligible from age sixty and is based on the number of years of a common-law partnership or marriage.

DTC, the Disability Tax Credit

The DTC is for those with a health condition (disability) who need ongoing health care/support. This is something you need to initiate with your physician or health care practitioner. The physician fills out a form providing the required details of your disability and then you will submit the form to the government for approval of this tax credit, which is $9,428 for 2023.

Examples are a child or dependent with epilepsy or cystic fibrosis, or an adult child needing continuing care, where the parent would apply for the DTC. Breathing trouble or hearing or incontinence issues also fall under this tax credit.

Additional to the DTC, there is a caregiver amount (this is a fairly new change in Canadian tax law— about three years old). You might qualify as the dependent's caregiver if, as with several of my clients, you are caring for a disabled adult child in the home. You need to be performing actions for the disabled individual.

REAL PEOPLE: DTC and Caregiver Stipend

One client of mine had a thirty-year-old disabled son living in the home with him and his wife. The son's income was less than $25,000, and their son was getting the Disability Tax Credit. They applied, proving the dependency that they were their son's caregivers and received an additional caregiver amount to help cover some of their costs.

REAL PEOPLE: Elder Qualification

I had an eighty-eight-year-old client come in to complete his taxes. He had not been our client up until then. He clearly used and needed a hearing aid to hear anything at all and a cane to walk safely. It is unknown why his previous tax preparer did not ask questions about his disabilities and look into the DTC for him. It is also unclear why his physician did not mention this eligibility to his patient (then again, they don't always). However, that was the case, so we not only applied for the DTC for the current tax year but applied for an adjustment extending back the allowed ten years. The government allowed the back payments, which gave him a nice tax-free lump sum that year. It was well worth the few dollars the doctor charged to fill out the forms.

Tax and Your Retirement Income

What are the effects of taxation on your available retirement income? Most of my clients just don't know! Come and sit with me to find out. When you start taking RRSPs sooner rather than later (or vice versa), it will affect your tax picture.

I see people retiring in their early sixties and taking their RRSPs. The latest age to take money out of the RRSP is age seventy-one. I advise all my clients to think more strategically about taking this money out.

In Canada, as an example of the tax impact, when the husband dies, his RRSP amount rolls over to his surviving spouse tax-free. Fast forward to when his wife dies. Whatever money is left is all taxable. This could represent several hundred thousand taxable dollars left in the account that their estate owes tax on.

You don't want this money to grow and accumulate too long, too much. This is why I look at each client's tax picture very closely with them.

Unlocking Your LIRA

A LIRA, Locked-In Retirement Account, is a special type of investment account for Canadians looking toward retirement.

If, during your working years, you are contributing to a Registered Pension Plan and leave that employer through a job change or retirement, the money in the RPP must be placed into a LIRA.

The issue can be getting the money out of the LIRA. You can start withdrawing from, or "unlocking," your LIRA between ages fifty-five to seventy-one. I encourage my clients to start withdrawing sooner rather than later.

Let's take an example of $100,000 just for simplicity. You have this accumulated in your LIRA, and you are fifty-five. You unlock 50 percent and then put $50,000 into an RRSP so the money is accessible at any time; the money is all taxable but you can access it at any time.

The other $50,000 goes into a LIF (Life Income Fund). You can withdraw only $3,500 or 7 percent per year of your $50,000 from the LIF. That is not very much money!

Here is why starting to withdraw it sooner is better. Take the same scenario I described above. Upon your death, your estate—your heirs—would potentially have a very large tax bill on the lump sum remaining in your LIF. By taking the allowed amount starting, for example, at age fifty-five, most people have withdrawn all the money by the time of their death.

REAL PEOPLE: Knowing If and When You Can Retire

A delightful longtime client of mine, Betty, is not the most organized person. She came in and told me the management at her workplace was pressuring her to retire. Then Betty commented that she couldn't afford to retire yet. I already knew this was not the case, so I said to her, "I'll bet you're only working for a few extra bucks a month." We made an appointment to look through her pension statements so I could prove to her that she could indeed afford to retire.

Betty was eligible for CPP. I demonstrated to her, by the numbers, that she was still going to work for only fifty dollars extra per week. She was resisting retirement over a matter of $200 a month.

On top of that, Betty paid ninety dollars per month just to park when she went to work. Then I figured out how much she was spending a month in gas just to get to work. As it happened, she was going to work—for free!

Another client, Rafe, had decided to work for a couple more years. He likewise was working for only $200 more a month. His rationale was that he hadn't worked for thirty years toward a full pension (not true, actually). Rafe was approaching age sixty-five. He already qualified for CPP and was just a couple of months away from qualifying for OAS; he was recently approved for the DTC after learning about this tax credit from our initial meeting.

In his mind, he thought working more would gain him a bigger pension. However, he had health issues, and his wife really hoped Rafe could afford to retire within the next couple of years. They both knew the job was beating up on his health. His wife was thrilled when I calculated his retirement income—and he happily retired immediately.

Between tax calculations and credits, people just don't know how to do the math and determine their needs, retirement income, and when they should retire. The disconnect in knowledge for most people is understanding the tax credits and the basic amounts. Almost no one has to earn as much "gross" income in retirement as when they are working. I am quite happy to help them understand those numbers and all of the advantages and benefits.

REAL PEOPLE: Time to Leave the Stress Behind

I have a longtime acquaintance named Dorothy who was not initially a client. She often expressed her dislike of her high-stress professional job at the hospital. She was worn out by the doom and gloom. When she spoke about it, you could plainly see she wanted out. Dorothy was approaching age sixty-five and had a hospital pension plan.

Her longtime financial advisor was another friend of hers, but knowing me as well, she came in to see me for a second opinion on her ability to retire.

I examined Dorothy's pension statements and plugged in all the numbers to demonstrate how her retirement would look with the basic amounts, credits, CPP, OAS, and her hospital pension. The bottom line showed her she was working for $44 per month! She was dumbfounded. It was quite comical to see! I imagined she would be swinging from a chandelier for days! That is how thrilled she was to leave her high-stress job.

Seeing this kind of reaction is why I choose to work with this age group. It is a pleasure to show them that after decades of hard work and saving, they can indeed retire comfortably.

The friend who was Dorothy's longtime financial advisor simply never ran those numbers for her. While she was prepared to work for two or more years, she immediately retired after submitting a month's notice.

Interest Income

What many Canadians do not know is that when they have interest income, they pay tax based on their marginal tax rate. A few examples of investments paying you interest income are:

- Traditional savings accounts
- Bonds
- T-Bills
- GICs or Guaranteed Interest Account (with an insurance carrier)

The problem is most of these instruments over the past twenty or so years have only paid out between 1–2 percent. If we use a more generous number of 2 percent and assume you have $100,000 in a traditional savings account, you will receive a tax slip for $2,000. In other words, $2,000 is taxable, but not as a "stand-alone" amount. The $2,000 gets tacked on to your total income, and you are paying tax on that new amount of money based on your marginal tax rate.

It is important to maximize your TFSAs. In the above example, maximizing the TFSA would be a great way to decrease or potentially eliminate your hefty tax bill.

REAL PEOPLE: GIC and Interest

How does that look? I prepared a tax return for a lady in her early nineties, and she had a tax slip for over $13,000 of interest income.

She had never owed tax in the preceding ten years and was quite upset when I explained to her that we had to include the $13,000 of income on her tax return. It appeared that she had a number of Guaranteed Investment Certificates (GICs), all of which were renewable in the same year. She apparently was aware of this, but not of the tax consequences.

I suggested she consider a laddering strategy. This is making sure your various GICs come up after one year, two years, three years, four years, and five years. The tax bill would look very different each year — advantageously so.

I asked if she had a TFSA, and she said she had about $25,000 in one. The problem there is the TFSA limit was $81,500 at the time I met with her. I suggested she speak with the bank or a financial advisor like me (remember — I was just doing her taxes) to make sure she has her TFSA maxed out. This would decrease the likelihood of an ugly tax bill in the future like the one she had just received.

Minimizing Dividends

If you are planning for retirement and concerned that you may have your Guaranteed Income Supplement (GIS) clawed back in the future, consider minimizing the amount of dividends you receive.

If your income is going to be higher and you are concerned about your Old Age Security (OAS) being clawed back, you may likewise want to consider minimizing the amount of dividends you receive.

In Canada, if you receive a dividend from a public corporation of $100, for example, you have to gross up that amount by 38 percent. So even though you receive just the $100, you have to report your total income as $138 on your tax return. You then get a tax credit of 15 percent or $15, based on the $100.

However, for purposes of calculating your total income, it can drastically increase your total if you have received a lot of dividend income. This is something that should be taken into consideration when planning your retirement income sources.

Capital Gains Spread

If you are considering a larger purchase, such as a vehicle, cottage, home, boat, etc., and you are going to be withdrawing money from a Non-Registered Account, you may want to consider withdrawing the money over two tax years if you can. This is a strategy that mitigates the tax impact.

REAL PEOPLE: Splitting Withdrawals over Two Tax Years

Capital gains tax can take a chunk of your profits right out of your pocket. Spread out the capital gain—and the taxes—over two years.

How does this look? I recently met with a gentleman named Samuel who was going to help his daughter Beth purchase a home after her divorce. I suggested Sam stagger his withdrawals over two tax years, rather than pulling out the whole amount he was going to use at one time.

When I met with Sam, it was in October, and Beth was still in the preliminary stages of looking for a house. She was still a few months out from purchasing a property. I knew this might just be perfect for him.

When I ran the tax liability numbers for Samuel in two scenarios (withdrawing it all now versus withdrawing in two parts over two tax years), the benefit of the latter option was crystal clear to him. Luckily, he and Beth had plenty of time for the strategy. It was year-end, so he modified his original plan, withdrew a portion right then, and the remainder at the beginning of the new year.

Now obviously, depending on the size of your purchase and the time of year, this may not be possible. In more cases than you think, this could definitely save you a lot of money by spreading a capital gain over more than one tax year. Come see me, and I'll run the numbers for you.

REAL PEOPLE: Monthly or One Lump Sum

A client of mine, Mikael, is leaving his job. He has an option of taking a set amount of monthly pension payments for life or taking a lump sum amount from his pension with no further future payment due to him. The lump sum is called a CV, or Commuted Value, of his pension.

This is another case where you need a professional to help you calculate the tax ramifications of taking the Commuted Value. It is also a matter of properly timing the decision.

Mikael could roll some of the CV into a LIRA and an RRSP account and take some as cash. I ran the numbers and showed him how this latter option, effective on January 1, would save him $30,000 in taxes rather than retiring on December 15 of the previous year.

Time your departure if it's voluntary resignation—and save taxes. Talk to me about how to use timing.

Chapter 4

Insulate Your Income

As you approach retirement and during retirement, you need a plan to protect your money with different investments and instruments than you might have had while you were working and saving.

You need to protect your nest egg from unforeseeable personal events or life changes like accidents and injuries, such as:

- A long-term recovery from an accident

- A fall resulting in a broken hip

- An auto accident or being hit by a car in a crosswalk, suffering broken bones, crushed ribs, and a major concussion

While accidents are impossible to predict, another kind of personal issue is also hard to predict: a chronic, long-term health issue requiring expensive care over many months or years. Major chronic diseases include:

- Cardiopulmonary (heart or lung) disease
- Diabetes
- Alzheimer's (cognitive disorders)
- Parkinson's
- Cancer

Perhaps a spouse cannot care for you, so you pay for a personal support worker to come into your home or go into a long-term care facility.

At age fifty-five, with a retirement goal of sixty, you don't have time to rebuild the cash amounts you took out for a disability costing you money.

If you have a gambling or other addiction that eats up your savings—beware! Your retirement funds are at risk. I had a client who did not know about her spouse's gambling habit until her home had no electricity. He wasn't paying the bills but using the money to bet.

If you can't say no to your kids—stop! Stop your habit to "help them out" by paying for their smartphone bills every month (and an up-to-the-minute new phone), or funding their auto insurance, or paying off credit cards or personal debts. I had a client who wanted to "help" his two kids pay back college debts and also buy each one a new car as a "graduation gift." Stop! Let them "adult" themselves into solvency! Your financial comfort in retirement will thank you.

How to Insulate Your Income

Having a good disability and critical illness insurance policy is essential for getting the best care but also for protecting your nest egg from large out-of-pocket medical expenses. You need to review your life insurance coverage and long-term care policies. Are your policies and beneficiaries up to date?

REAL PEOPLE: Life Insurance Solutions at Any Age

When one spouse dies, the survivor is left with 50 percent of the pre-death income. You might get a 60 percent survivor's pension, but that still might not be enough to live a comfortable retirement—or provide all your needs before retirement, for that matter.

A solution is life insurance.

Lucille is a spouse who stays at home with four children under the age of seven. Steve, her husband, works a good-paying job.

Each one needed more substantial life insurance of the appropriate type. Steve did not understand why Lucille would need just as much life insurance coverage as he did. After all, he was the earner, and he needed his policy to cover the earnings that would be lost for the household. Why did Lucille need just as much insurance?

I explained that if Lucille were to pass away, Steve would not be quitting his job to take care of the four children. He agreed. I pointed out that he would need to hire a regular childcare provider, perhaps someone to transport his children to and from school morning and afternoon, do their family grocery shopping, take the kids to doctor appointments, and sit with the older children after school to supervise their homework while waiting for Steve to get home from work.

Did he think his current income could pay what might be a full-time salary for people to provide these services in the case of Lucille's death? That woke him up! As long as you have dependent children, you need to have life insurance in the right amounts.

An employer may offer some life insurance; you may have to subscribe to more. You should re-evaluate your coverage every two years or so. Talk to me, as I am life insurance licensed.

Long-term care, LTC, is also insurance. In Canada, there are only two carriers. (This type of coverage is, alas, going by the wayside because of the amount of claims so the cost of the coverage keeps increasing.) It can protect your family's retirement assets if you can qualify and one of the limited products suits your needs.

Save as much money as possible. Some employers offer short- and long-term disability coverage to cover two-thirds of your income in income protection coverage.

REAL PEOPLE: Beneficiary Review

I had a couple, Jeff and Jen, who had been married for seven years. He still had his sister as a beneficiary on his policies; he had simply forgotten about the policies.

I find most people have, on average, about five financial accounts they need to check in on any time there are life changes. Make it a habit to check on those accounts and policies annually, and you won't miss any life changes.

Work-life insurance policies, personally owned life insurance policies, TFSA, RRSP, and work-registered accounts are the typical beneficiary accounts to look at and keep up-to-date.

Chapter 5

Reinforce Your Wealth

In Chapter 4, I talked about what personal or health events and changes can devastate and decimate your life savings and affect the quality of your retirement years.

Now let's look at the external changes that can also reduce your nest egg—and that you can protect against.

The world didn't see what effects the March 2000 dot-com crash, the following year's 9/11 attack and immediate market disruptions, or the 2020 COVID-19 pandemic would have on our savings and earning power. Before COVID (and even during its first year), no one saw any inflation. It wasn't on anyone's radar.

Before any of these "sudden" external events, you could have had a plush portfolio going. You could have grown your initial savings into a ton of money. Then, BAM! Your portfolio value plummets 50 percent.

> **Don't roll your eyes. Don't say, "It won't happen to me." It has happened—look at the stock exchange charts.**

Market risk and inflation risk are two types of risk that can affect your retirement lifestyle. Banks are good at scaring people about market risks. But as I've said elsewhere, they are not very good about talking about inflation risk. If all your money in the markets goes down the tube in a market crash, you could well outlive your money. If inflation persists and eats away at your purchasing power, you'll need to spend more dollars for the same lifestyle, and again, you might just outlive your money.

At age fifty-five, with a retirement goal of sixty, you don't have time to watch markets rise again to bring your accounts back to the earlier high amounts. During retirement, you have zero time to recoup losses; you need that money coming in every month.

Liquidity risk is also a consideration. As an example, if your money is locked up in four- and five-year GICs (Guaranteed Investment Certificates) at the bank, what do you do if you need cash right away? That money is not liquid. You cannot cash them out as they are typically non-redeemable during the term of the GIC.

Protect your current nest egg from being whittled away by markets and the economy. Make sure enough of your assets are liquid so you are not forced into taking out a line of credit at age eighty-two for your long-term care bills.

Don't let your hard-earned nest egg dwindle. It is about structure and protection. Any market portfolio needs regular monitoring for performance, and "regular" means an annual review at the bare minimum before retirement and quarterly once you are retired.

You need to be in the right type of investments, which are also right for your degree of risk tolerance, your age, and your future cash needs. Many bank advisors don't ever go that deep in their discussions with you. Don't assume your non-bank financial advisor will proactively bring up this range of topics either, much less that he will even call you to make an appointment. Make the appointment yourself—even if you don't see any particular market changes. The markets are volatile, and you don't want to suffer a down market just when you need that money.

Segregated Funds

This is a mutual fund with an insurance wrapper. It is sold only by an insurance company. The huge advantage is that the initial principal is protected by a death benefit guarantee.

The difference between buying a segregated fund and buying a straight mutual fund at your bank is volatility protection. What if, for example, market volatility reduces your fund from the initial $100,000 invested to around $80,000, and you were to pass away? Your bank would only pay out the fair market value of $80,000 to your beneficiary. However, with a segregated fund, your beneficiary would receive the initial $100,000 that you invested.

This solution costs a little more in upfront costs because of a higher management fee, but it is well worth it in a volatile market environment.

Another benefit: The money stays out of probate (hence the term "segregated" or "separate" from the individual's other assets). In Ontario, the authorities want to know your net worth and the probate fees will be 15 percent of that amount. A segregated fund is outside of probate—segregated from your other assets—and saves you the fees.

REAL PEOPLE: Saving Thousands in Probate Fees

I had a family come to see me in 2021. Patricia, the mother, had been diagnosed with stage 4 lung cancer. Unfortunately, the prognosis was not good but we had the benefit of some time to ensure that her affairs were in order. Patricia brought her two grown children, Jason and Jamie, to the initial appointment. Patricia had over $200,000 in a RRIF with her bank, along with over $100,000 in a TFSA and almost $100,000 in a savings account. I suggested that we move the RRIF and TFSA funds into a segregated fund and the bulk of the savings into a Guaranteed Interest Account. Patricia named Jason and Jamie as beneficiaries on the account.

Patricia passed away a few months later. Jason called me to thank me because all they had to worry about paying probate fees on was Patricia's principal residence. Patricia moved almost $400,000 into segregated funds, and this allowed the money to stay outside of her estate. Not only did Jason and Jamie receive the funds within two weeks of Patricia passing away, but they also received $6,000 more collectively because they saved $15 per $1,000 ($400,000 x .15) in probate fees.

Annuities

These give a predictable, guaranteed income stream. They are insurance products in Canada. They offer payout flexibility to suit your needs. You can have a "ten-year term certain" and many other payout solutions to choose from.

The payout represents a predictable and guaranteed income stream for you.

REAL PEOPLE: Additional Protection and Invisibility

Segregated Funds are creditor-protected. This can be a great additional advantage. I've had a number of clients who have been sued (life happens), and as we had segregated some funds, they were not affected. No one can take those assets from you.

My client Stephanie was diagnosed with terminal brain cancer at a time the markets had gone down, and the segregated fund death benefit topped up her funds for her family.

Once a will has been probated, anyone can view it as a public document at the city office. Segregated funds will not be visible in such documents.

Marilyn was a client in a relationship with an overly controlling spouse. She had a beloved granddaughter to whom she wanted to leave a legacy with no pushback from her spouse. I set up a segregated fund amount with the granddaughter as the sole beneficiary. Marilyn's spouse didn't know about it, but even if he had, there would be no action he could ever take to change it.

I'm insurance licensed, and I can offer my clients instruments to protect them that they won't be able to get at their bank or other types of financial institutions. Come and consult me about some options.

Cash Flow Security

Could you outlive your money? This is a fear in many people's minds before they pull the trigger and retire. It is why sitting with me is so valuable (and a big stress reliever!) to my clients. I know how to analyze your cash flow.

The term "cash flow" means you have the cash in hand to cover your needs, month after month. It means you have assets that are quickly convertible to cash. Convertibility means your shares in your stock portfolio can be turned into cash in one day; your monthly pension payment comes to you like clockwork as cash. On the other hand, a piece of real estate cannot be turned into cash overnight because of the long process to sell and realize the funds from the sale.

Cash flow is an issue to pay attention to throughout your retirement, primarily due to inflation and surprise needs for cash (typically for medical or health care issues that arise).

REAL PEOPLE: **Cash Flow and Medical Expenses**

A client's seventy-year-old Canadian friend, Stephen, was in the US for a vacation and fell ill there, landing in the local hospital. His money in Canada at his credit union (due to how the CU set up his accounts) was not liquid, i.e., not easily accessible as cash. American hospitals want proof of ability to pay for services and care, even from foreign visitors in distress. Stephen had to jump through a bunch of hoops, including applying for a line of credit in the US to pay for his expensive hospital care.

Make sure you have money that is accessible; don't be concerned about the bank's best interest but your own.

Inflation eats away at your cash so you need to update your plan every year. This means having different pots of money you can take cash from as prices rise over time. This helps maintain your standard of living. Have conservative, protected investments as opposed to lots of money in the volatile markets.

Inflation is also the primary reason you need to consult with a trusted financial advisor throughout your retirement years about cash flow. Clearly, we do not have a crystal ball to predict how much inflation will affect your nest egg for the next twenty-five or thirty years. However, we have access to information and calculators to help you prepare for inflation as you move through your retirement. Come and ask me about this.

REAL PEOPLE: Longevity and Outliving Your Money

You need to look at your financial preparation to cover long-term health care costs. As an example, if your financial picture allows you to pay for a long-term facility for fourteen years, but you live longer than that, how will your remaining years in the facility be paid? Do you have children who can afford to pay your costs after the fourteen years are up? This is a calculation you need to look at closely. I can help you run the numbers and look at your options.

At this writing, I have one client named Don, who pays about $6,000 a month to reside and receive needed care in his chosen facility. Fourteen years is just about how long Don's money would last at that level of spending, based on his pension and his savings.

He is disappointed he cannot now afford to pay for a grandchild's education (as he had hoped) because he needs to pay his own increased costs of living.

Chapter 6

Establish Your Legacy

How do you want to be remembered?

My grandfather died when I was seventeen and left me $5,000. It was a huge amount to me! I was able to buy myself my first car. I still remember the feelings; it was because of his legacy to me.

There are various ways you can create your legacy without leaving a cash amount to someone as my grandfather did.

Types of Legacy

One of my clients created an annual family event (like a reunion) during her seventies. She left money earmarked for food and entertainment so the family could carry on the tradition after her death. Another client of mine had two kids and five grandkids. She left money to them all in a segregated fund, along with a separate bequest to a hospice. She detailed these bequests in her will. Yet another client funded a bench at his favorite park with his name on it. Others have created scholarships or funded rooms in hospitals.

Leaving money to a charity by bequeathing stock market shares, a life insurance benefit, and property are all ways some of my clients have created a legacy and benefited from tax advantages.

Legacies are as unique as you are. How do you wish to be remembered?

Who Will Your Legacy Support?
For Your Special-Needs Dependent

The Henson Trust is a special way to protect your assets for a family member with a mental or physical disability, beyond the Ontario Disability Support Payments (ODSP).

However (and again, this is for Ontario), if a parent dies and leaves more than $100,000 outright to a disabled child, the ODSP benefit goes away. You might believe the large sum of cash you leave will be enough. Don't assume this! Having a lawyer establish a Henson Trust protects the child's inheritance in full while also protecting his ODSP benefit.

How to Use Life Insurance for a Legacy

Needs change throughout life as far as life insurance goes. When you are young, you get it as protection for income replacement, a mortgage, and your family when you have dependents.

Later, as your children move out of the house, you have insurance to cover the costs of your funeral. But you might also want to make sure there is money to help pay for weddings, higher education, or special-needs family members (so they can afford care for their whole life).

You might want to ensure that your money goes to the next generation tax-free or the charity of your choice. Name a beneficiary on your insurance policy. You can spell out in a will how the money is to be used.

We have a gradual inheritance strategy or annuity settlement option (gradual payout of the sum) to help you "help" your heirs. If you have a granddaughter to whom you can and wish to leave $1,000,000—yet do not wish for her to have the whole sum at once—use a gradual inheritance strategy. It might pay her $20,000 a year until the policy runs out.

Don't Give It All in One Lump Sum

One of my older clients, Frances, had eight adult kids. Two of them drank heavily and gambled addictively. Understanding their lifestyles, she set the policies up using the gradual inheritance strategy or annuity settlement option. Frances and her late husband worked very hard to accumulate their investment assets.

Naturally, all her kids clamored for her to bequeath the entire lump sum to them at one time. The kids complained and threatened to call a lawyer if she didn't.

Well, I laughed and got Frances laughing, too. Why? Insurance companies have battalions of lawyers. Even though my client understood that her children would be unable to change her policies, their behavior prompted her to set up policies with gradual payout strategies—for all of them! Although the grown children didn't see it at the time, Frances really did give them a gift by paying the funds to them over time.

Setting this up through an insurance carrier's policy is best; that way you don't have to change your will every time there is some life event. When new grandkids come along, you reallocate the money versus paying a lawyer to redo your will with such changes.

You could set up a trust to achieve this, but it is a less expensive process through an insurance carrier.

Cascading

More affluent people with lots of additional cash flow want to put their money somewhere else. Parents can buy a policy on their own life with their child as the beneficiary; this is fairly traditional.

There is another option. It is a three-generation setup called cascading. Grandma owns and pays for the policy to insure her child's life as a contingent owner, naming her grandchild as the beneficiary. Even when Grandma dies, her child takes over ownership of the policy, which remains intact for the grandchild.

Leave a Legacy, Not a Mess

Planning for retirement is not only about having enough money for all the years of your life. It can be about leaving a legacy.

You don't want your legacy to be that "Dad left a real mess of paperwork!" or "Whew, Mom sure didn't have her assets well-documented!" Legacies call for some reorganization and planning, just as your financial foundation does. This planning is about not leaving a mess for your family, beneficiaries, and heirs upon your death.

You have earned and saved all this money; you have done all this financial planning work up to this point. Now you need to attend to some legal planning so that when you are gone, things are straightforward for every loved one you leave behind.

The Importance of a Will and POA

If you own any type of asset—real estate, a business, valuable (and insured) jewelry, cash accounts, RVs, or other vehicles, etc.—you need a will. A lawyer needs to draft it for you. This is not a do-it-yourself document!

A will is a legally binding document that tells the authorities, the executor of your estate, and all of your loved ones and beneficiaries how to dispose of your property upon your death.

When you are a parent with minor children, you draft a will. Its intent is usually about the care of your children in the event of your death while they are still underage. A will is also important, whatever your age might be, if you have disabled adult children still in your care.

REAL PEOPLE: Structuring to Save on Probate Fees

A GIA, Guaranteed Interest Account, is similar to the GIC at your bank, but is issued by an insurance carrier. Money in a GIA sits outside probate and has creditor protection since it is not visible to anyone looking into your probate settlement.

A client named Roberta had $200,000 in the bank. We transferred her money into a high-interest savings account with an insurance policy and a GIA—it is all kept outside of probate. It is, however, still accessible if Roberta ever needs it.

REAL PEOPLE: Common-Law Partner vs. Marriage

In my province, common-law partners have very few rights.

Rita had been with her common-law partner, Mark, for eight years when he died. Mark died intestate, which means he had no will. Because of that, his assets went to his children. Rita was left in the cold, literally, since Mark's daughter immediately kicked her out of the house they had been living in.

The daughter gave Rita the statutory thirty days to vacate the home. Not only was Rita mourning her late partner, but she also had no home, no rights to any of his assets, and no recourse. If Mark had drawn up a will, he could have left her everything, and it would have been his daughter and other children who had no recourse to change things.

The Power of Attorney (POA)

A Power of Attorney (POA) is a binding legal document. This legal document authorizes an individual or corporate trustee (such as a legal firm or bank) to make decisions on your behalf. The types of decisions the designated individual can make are specified in this document.

You may have heard the term "executor." The main difference between an executor and a POA is that the POA may act during your lifetime on your behalf, while an executor steps in upon your death to fulfill the terms of your will.

A POA is of two types in Canada:

1. Personal Care. In case of your incapacity due to an accident or long-term illness, the POA

grants the ability to the named individual to make medical decisions concerning you. If you do not have a POA and a family member is not present to make such decisions, the hospital will make medical decisions in your best interests.

2. Property Care. Property here means all your assets. This individual is authorized to make your payments or banking in your place. This POA can be active even when you are not incapacitated—in other words, you do not have to be ill or otherwise incapacitated at all.

If you are a business owner, you should have a separate will for this asset. Often your incorporation or your partnership agreement places your business outside of your will. If not, consider drafting two separate wills.

Choosing Your POA

The person or institution you name as your POA has a lot of power so be sure you trust them. Choose wisely. Remember, a POA is in effect during your lifetime. You don't want this person (or institution's personnel) to walk off with all your assets or mismanage them so you are left destitute. One key to choosing the right person is making sure he or she is up to the task. You need to know that this person can take care of your affairs.

Upon your death, your Executor will become responsible for filing all your tax returns in Canada and other countries where you are liable for taxes for the current and all past years you may not have filed. The Executor will be closing out all your investment accounts. An Executor may potentially be involved with your disgruntled family, so this person might need to be thick-skinned and not take complaints personally.

Life is full of changes. Update your will, your life insurance policies, and your POA designations. Take a new look at your beneficiaries. Every time you have a life event happen—a divorce, a remarriage, the birth of a child, the death of a beneficiary, or an investment in or divestment of your assets—you need to do this. Especially once you get older, do this check-in once or twice a year, just like changing your home's smoke alarm batteries!

The Future Value of Your Estate

In leaving legacies, I encourage my clients to consider the future value of their estate.

Project the values of your assets as you prepare for retirement and during your retirement. Many people retire and live for another thirty years. History shows us that real estate values, the value of gold or silver, and the valuation of businesses all rise and fall. How might your assets' values rise or fall before your death? How might they be leveraged to supplement your income in the future?

I am often asked, "What about putting my kids' names on a house or bank account?" This is different from naming them as your POA. I get asked about this all the time when individuals get older.

> **The answer is not easy but there are some things to consider.**

First, are your children trustworthy? Do they have the capacity to manage those assets for you if needed — rather than mismanage them?

Next are the tax implications. If thirty years ago, you invested $200,000 in a lakefront cottage, and it's worth $1.2 million today, you will have to discuss the tax implications of selling it. If it is not your primary residence, the tax will be owed! If you still own it upon your death, your beneficiaries will owe tax on the capital gain when they sell it. But how much? Unless you organize your finances properly and have a discussion with a financial planner like me, you may not know until it is too late to adjust. I do this kind of calculation and tax estimation for clients all the time.

Such a discussion also helps you make sure what your financial position is if you sell a primary residence and downsize to something cheaper at the time of retirement. What is the tax implication on profits you've made, and how much is left to plump up your retirement funds? Ask me.

This asset and tax discussion also clarifies your legacy to beneficiaries. If you had planned to leave property to one or more children, how can you structure it so they do not lose the benefit of the inheritance through a huge tax bill? Your family will thank you for structuring your assets properly.

My strong advice: Take care of your assets year after year and not just on a once-and-done basis. Take care of how you structure your legacy, through the will and the POA, and make sure your advisor is giving you complete information about your assets, cash flow, tax picture, legacy, and all your options.

If your advisor doesn't keep in touch with you, change advisors. They are paid to do this type of analysis, follow-ups, and corrections. However, you need to be in touch, too, with them to get this done.

REAL PEOPLE: A Deed Gone Wrong

Twenty years ago, Jasper and Reine put their two kids on the deed of their primary residence with them. They had imagined leaving the property to their two children in equal shares upon their death and wanted to avoid probate and the associated $15 per $1,000 fees.

Fast forward, and Jasper and Reine are both in a long-term care facility. They sold the house while they were alive. They bought it at $200,000 and sold it for $800,000. The couple had no capital gains tax on their respective 25 percent gain because it was their primary residence. Both children, however, owned other property as their primary residences. When this sale went through, each child, therefore, owed tax on their respective $150,000 capital gain. It turned out not to be such a great windfall for the kids. The 25 percent gain needed to be declared as taxable income by each child, probably adding an extra $25,000 each on their tax bills that year. Thankfully the children did not have any marital or financial issues during the time their names were on the home. Had one of the children gotten divorced or been sued, then that would have also added in another layer of complexity.

Putting your child's name on your bank accounts is a bit different, but can be just as risky. Or more so! The ease of paying bills draws elder people to this solution, so they add their adult child's name to the account and hand the checkbook over to them. However, the temptation to drain their mom's or dad's bank account is real, as in, "My folks would have wanted me to have some/all of this cash to do _____." There are many court cases dealing with just this scenario.

Like naming an Executor or POA, you have to trust the named individual. The tax picture requires the POA to get expert advice. There is a probate process to understand. Does your POA understand all the fiscal and legal obligations? Also, keep in mind that family members are not always close at hand. We are a mobile people. If your preferred executor lives outside the country or across the continent, you might consider another individual for the job.

Deemed Disposition and Final Taxes

Structure things properly. If the husband dies, money in the RRSP or RRIF rolls over tax-free to the surviving spouse. When the surviving spouse passes away, the tax authorities apply the principle of deemed disposition. This is the fair market value of the account on the day the wife died; the money value is what the authorities calculate tax on. Is there money available for that tax bill?

> JUST A NOTE: *Spousal rollovers are not always the best option.*

Is your sale of an asset (a business or piece of property) going to generate a capital gain, and if so, what are the other tax implications? What are the ways to mitigate the tax picture?

Intermission

RETIRE: **In the preceding chapters, I have presented the six core considerations for your retirement preparation.**

They ask you to:

Review Your Foundation

Envision Your Future

Trim Your Taxes

Insulate Your Income

Reinforce Your Wealth

Establish Your Legacy

Taking care of these six areas properly requires professional guidance for most people. I am happy to consult with you to review your financial organization and make recommendations to you. Indeed, simply reorganizing your finances can take care of most of your concerns for your retirement years.

However, I advise most people to go further and create a formalized financial plan for their retirement. In the next chapter, I will show you how that looks by telling you the stories of three of my actual clients.

Chapter 7

The Importance of Having a Plan

In my twenty years as a financial advisor, I have met with thousands of clients and prospective clients. The one thing that I really hope you take away from this book is the importance of *having a retirement plan*.

It is important to have an advisor who has created a plan with you. DIY, or do-it-yourself, plans run the risk of missing lots of advantages and benefits.

REAL PEOPLE: **Jane**

I had a meeting with Jane a few weeks ago. I have known Jane's husband for a number of years, and he knows I am a financial advisor. He reached out a couple of times with some quick questions but finally decided to ask me if I would mind meeting with them to review their financial situation. They decided they needed to make sure they were on track.

They gave me a few details ahead of our appointment so I was able to prepare. When I met with them, I asked what Jane's take-home pay was; it averaged $1,800 biweekly. She had just turned sixty-five.

I prepared a mock tax return for her. I showed her what things would look like if she were to retire and take her defined benefit pension amount of $3,120 per month. I told her what her full Canada Pension amount would be. Plus, because she is sixty-five and was born and raised in Canada, she is eligible for full Old Age Security (OAS). Therefore, I added that income in as well.

I explained that in Canada, there is no tax on the first $15,000 of income anyone makes. She is eligible for the age amount because she is sixty-five. However, because her income is over the $39,826, that means that she gets a portion of the $8,396 age amount which, in Jane's case, is $4,615.

It got better. I also explained, because she would be receiving pension income, she is eligible for a $2,000 pension credit.

I explained that Jane could make $21,615 before she had to pay any tax. I added up the defined benefit payment she could receive from her pension, her Canada Pension, and her Old Age Security, and plugged that total into a tax return.

We calculated what her biweekly amount would be in retirement. I used a biweekly amount because that is how she was used to being paid all those years.

The shocker? She was essentially working for $22.00 biweekly, so we'll call it $44 per month. There were about two minutes of pure silence with Jane just staring at me with her mouth open. The look on her face clearly said, "What the ****?" What she actually said was, "No way!"

So I explained it to her again and said, "I think you can retire now; you don't have to continue working. My guess is, based on the proximity of your house to your job, you very likely spend more than $44.00 per month on gas, not to mention the fact you told me how incredibly stressful your job is. With these numbers? You can retire."

I'm not sure if you remember an old commercial where a guy walking around off-balance is told he should have had his vegetables, then he gets bonked in the head with a V8 bottle. It was one of those "Holy cow, what am I doing?" moments for Jane.

Jane has had the same financial advisor for almost twenty years at the same institution, and the advisor is also a friend. By the time our meeting was done, Jane was asking me, "How do I transfer my investments to you to manage?" She could not believe she was sixty-five, still going to work, stressing, trying to figure out if she could retire potentially in two years, and here I am, showing her by the numbers that she was working for $11.00 per week!

From just a money standpoint, it was obviously a no-brainer. I said, "Hey, I'm pretty sure I'm going to leave here, and you guys are going to be swinging from the chandelier. Let this settle in. I know it's a lot of information to take in, and if you want to meet again in a week or two to go through this again, I'm more than happy to do that. I can clearly articulate it on paper at that time for you. But right now? Just let it sink in."

Fast forward a couple of months. Jane is now happily retired, enjoying spending time with her grandkids. She gave her company time to replace her because she was a diligent, valuable employee, a wonderful lady who wanted to make sure everything was covered before she left the job. No doubt about it—Jane is absolutely ecstatic that she is now retired.

This story emphasizes why it is important to have a plan. Can you imagine? Jane—and so many like her—would potentially have gone to work for an extra two plus years, simply because her advisor at the bank couldn't run the same retirement plan numbers I could.

REAL PEOPLE: **Bert**

The next story I would like to share is about a gentleman whom I will call Bert. Bert and his wife found me online. The funny thing is that I looked up Bert's wife, Ella, on Facebook, and it turned out Ella and I have about ten friends in common and most of them are my clients. Another funny thing is that we probably would have connected if she had asked someone for a referral, but she actually found me online looking for a financial advisor.

At the time of writing this book, I had about 170 positive Google reviews. Hopefully, by the time this book is published, there will be more. If they always bring clients like Ella and Bert to me, I will be happy!

Ella expressed that Bert had several health issues, including diabetes, and part of his foot had been amputated. Ella was really hoping Bert could retire soon and enjoy their life together as he has a fairly stressful job.

When they called to book the appointment, my assistant asked them to bring in a copy of their tax returns and investment statements.

I did a mock tax return for the following year to show Bert that, if he retired from being a civil servant, what his defined benefit pension plan would pay. He was also just a couple of months away from being eligible for a full Canada Pension. Because he was born and raised in Canada and is turning sixty-five in a few months, he would also be eligible for full Old Age Security (OAS).

My mock tax return showed his income from his Defined Benefit Pension, his Canada Pension, and his Old Age Security. The outcome was a very similar story to Jane's. I showed him what his take-home would be after tax on his pension income, and it was about $200 less than what he was taking home right now working full-time.

Bert and Ella were in the process of closing on the sale of their home. From the sale of the home, they would have over $400,000 of excess money they needed to do something with. I told them, even with $400,000 being extremely conservative, we could make sure he got at least $200 a month additional income—for life. In other words, we could most likely generate more than that from it. I just wanted them to know they would not be losing out on income if Bert retired right at age sixty-five.

Bert and Ella came back a couple of weeks later. The sale of the house closed, and we maxed out their TFSAs. We opened up a non-registered account. Bert told me he already had a resignation letter ready to go. Ella must have thanked me at least ten times at our second meeting—she was absolutely ecstatic and so appreciative of my help.

Ella also said, "You know, we've been at the same bank for a long time, and they've never given us this kind of information and planning. I had a very demanding job, and was always worrying about Bert." But now I have given her the gift of not worrying. Financially, they are retiring in comfort.

The message I really want you to take from these stories is to make sure you meet with somebody who knows the ins and outs of income taxes, knows how to do a retirement plan, and understands that a tax plan is absolutely imperative. Bert probably would have worked for at least two more years, and he would have been compromising his health for about $200 per month.

The next story I want to share is about Gina, who comes to mind because I had coffee with her today as I was writing this book.

I thought back to a few years ago when I said to Gina, "I don't know why you're continuing to work. You can retire." Gina retired, but a funny thing happened about six months later. She called me and said, "You know, Alynn, I have to apologize. You were so right! I could afford to retire. I make more money now than I did when I was working!"

I've been doing this for a long time. It's funny because I don't think people really understand how much money comes out of their cheques every single week when they are working.

Gina was a nurse and had a good-paying job, making on average $90,000 to $100,000 per year. But you can imagine with EI, CPP, and union dues coming out of her cheque, it deducted a lot of potential income. She also had professional dues she had to pay, based on her nursing credentials, which she paid out-of-pocket. She also had to pay into her Healthcare of Ontario Pension Plan (HOOPP) (defined benefit) pension plan out of her pay.

Gina didn't retire until she was nearly sixty-eight. She not only had more than thirty years of income as a nurse, but she also had a Canada Pension. It was a bit of an increased benefit because she waited until after age sixty-five to take it. Plus, she had an increased income from Old Age Security—again because she waited to take it. In retirement, she was actually taking home more money on HOOPP, Canada Pension, and Old Age (after tax) than she was taking home from her job. Not to mention we split a portion of her pension with her husband, so he also gets the $2,000 pension credit.

Gina said, "Oh, Alynn. I retired. I trusted you. I didn't really believe it until I saw I'm making more money now that I am retired than when I was actually working."

It's funny how we are wired. We can't fathom the idea of making more money in retirement than working. It's crazy how much money comes out of your cheque every single week when you're working. Because the money is gone without you ever touching it, you don't realize that when retired, there's not usually such a huge disparity.

It goes back to looking at what the basic limit is in Canada. If you're sixty-five or older, you're eligible for the age credit and the pension credit.

Obviously, this differs from sector to sector, but I have a number of clients who are in the nursing field, civil servants such as police officers who work for the City of Windsor where I live, and many teachers—all eligible for good pensions. When you're eligible for a good pension, you don't necessarily realize how many deductions are coming out of your pay during your working life. Knowing this and how to crunch those numbers is really what sets apart the planning I do from that of other advisors. You simply cannot do it yourself with the same accuracy (at least this is my observation after nearly twenty years in the field).

Taking a look at what you are going to take home is really the pivotal calculation. Looking at your retirement "take-home income," you will realize you can feel comfortable pulling the trigger and retiring. I've run the numbers for thousands of clients to show them with clarity how they can comfortably retire. Come and see me. I'll run the numbers for you.

Alynn Godfroy
Designations

My clients realize the financial planning industry is quite regulated. Part of that regulation is to ensure that advisors such as myself are fully trained and educated.

Much like a university diploma, when we have completed courses of education, we are awarded what is called a designation.

Advisors very rarely explain the value of these designations to their clients. I would like to do it here. Consulting with advisors who show these designations brings you many benefits.

Certified Financial Planner (CFP) Designation

The benefit to the client:
The most widely recognized financial planning designation in Canada and worldwide, the Certified Financial Planner® designation assures Canadians that the design of their financial future rests with a professional who will put their clients' interests ahead of their own.

There are approximately 17,000 CFP professionals across Canada, part of an international network of more than 175,000 CFP professionals in twenty-six territories around the world.

CFP certification is considered the standard for the financial planning profession worldwide. CFP professionals have demonstrated the knowledge, skills, experience, and ethics to examine their clients' entire financial picture at the highest level of complexity required of the profession and work with their clients to build a financial plan so they can *Live Life Confidently*™.

To obtain the CFP designation, candidates must complete a rigorous education program, pass a national exam, and demonstrate three years of qualifying work experience.

To maintain certification, CFP professionals must keep their knowledge and skills current by completing twenty-five hours of continuing education each year. They must also adhere to the FP Canada Standards Council™ *Standards of Professional Responsibility*, including a code of ethics which mandates CFP professionals place their clients' interests first. The Standards Council vigilantly enforces these standards.

Certified Life Underwriter (CLU) Designation

The benefit to the client:
This designation is for elite professional financial advisors who raise the bar in developing practical solutions for individuals, business owners, and professionals in risk management, wealth creation and preservation, estate planning, and wealth transfer.

Master Financial Advisor (MFA) Designation

The benefit to the client:
This is specialty training allowing us to address the financial and succession issues of the baby boomer demographic. It brings with it a heavy focus on Strategic Philanthropy, The Charitable Sector, and Gift Planning. There is also a large focus on pension benefits.

Elder Planning Counsellor (EPC) Designation

The benefit to the client:
This is specific training allowing us to work with the fifty-plus population to plan their current and future lives. This offers more to the client than just retirement planning; it's about being a financial advisor to someone close to, or in, retirement and continuing to work with them through the remainder of their life.

Certified Executor Advisors (CEA) Designation

The benefit to the client:
Executors of a will may have to work with up to seventeen different professionals in their duties. Certified Executor Advisors are experts in their field and can help you navigate all the challenges of dealing with multiple professionals. They can steer executors of wills away from potential problems and toward the professionals they need.

As a result, CEAs can offer tremendous value. They've seen what happens when estates are unprepared and the possible shocking fallout. The results can be estates frozen for years or sometimes decades, heirs who are disinherited, intended charitable bequests defeated, and families ripped apart permanently.

Alynn Godfroy Bio

Alynn Godfroy, an award-winning financial retirement specialist, is a tax expert recognized as one of the leading independent advisors in Southwestern Ontario. Her goal is to help Canadians plan correctly for retirement because she has witnessed the fallout for families unprepared for transitional periods such as retirement, succession, or the sudden loss of a loved one.

An admitted bookworm and nerd, she loves to increase her knowledge about all things financial. In 2020 alone, she accumulated over 290 continuing education hours—a spectacular achievement when her license requirement is only thirty hours *every year*.

Over the last twenty years, Alynn has acquired five specific financial retirement designations. This has established Godfroy Financial as the most *trusted source* for financial advice and one of the *most qualified* in Windsor/Essex County.

As an avid swimmer, her perfect day off consists of lounging around the pool with her son, Austin, and husband, Terry.

Her favourite movie is Dirty Dancing, and as the saying goes, "Nobody puts Baby in the corner." Well, Alynn's thought is, "Nobody puts retirees in the corner when it comes to their finances!"

Alynn is committed to helping her clients in these key areas: *Tax Optimization, Wealth Preservation, and Estate Planning.* In addition, Godfroy Financial offers you a complimentary second opinion on your financial plan.

Godfroy Financial
Phone: 519-258-1995
Email: *alynn@godfroyfinancial.com*

References
and Resources

Budget - Intake Form

Client Information

	You	Spouse
Name:		
Phone #:		

Income

	You		Spouse
Take Home Pay		ie. Weekly, bi-weekly etc	
# of pays/year			
Rental Income			
Child Benefits			
Alimony			
Child Support			
Pension(s)			
Other			
CPP/OAS			

Mortgage

		Assets	
Home Value		Cottage	
Balance		Vehicle # 1	
Payment		Vehicle # 2	
Frequency		Recreation Vehicle	
		Other	

Debts

Type of Debt	Lender	Limit	Balance	% Rate	Min Payment

Savings

	You	Spouse
RRSP	_____	_____
TFSA	_____	_____
RESP	_____	_____
Savings	_____	_____
Group Pension(s)	_____	_____
Stocks/mutual Funds	_____	_____
Other	_____	_____

Housing

Monthly Total

Condo Fees	_____
Cell Phone	_____
Heat / Gas	_____
Power / Hydro	_____
Water	_____
Property Tax	_____
House Insurance	_____
Phone Cable Internet	_____
Water Heater Rental	_____
Other Housing expenses	_____

Transportation

Monthly Total

Vehicle Lease	_____
Vehicle Loan	_____
Vehicle Loan	_____
Gas	_____
Maintenance/Repairs	_____
Parking	_____
Transit passes/Taxi	_____
Tolls	_____
Insurance	_____
Other/uber etc	_____

Financial Costs

Monthly Total

Alimony	_____
Child Support	_____
Child Care / Day Care	_____
Disability Insurance	_____
Life Insurance	_____
Health Insurance	_____
Long Term Care Ins.	_____
Interest Fees / Overdraft	_____
RRSP	_____
TFSA / IRA	_____
Pension	_____

RESP	_____
Other	_____
Other	_____

GODFROY FINANCIAL

Living Expenses

	Monthly Total		Monthly Total
Groceries	_____	Beer Store	_____
Dining / Eating Out	_____	Liquor / Wine Making	_____
Entertainment / Movies	_____	Smoking / Cigarettes	_____
Clothing	_____	Manicure/Pedi	_____
Jewelery	_____	Hair Cuts	_____
House Cleaning	_____	Lottery Tix/Casino/Bingo	_____
Fitness/Gym Memberships	_____	Sports - hockey/baseball etc.	_____
Health Care - Vitamins etc.	_____	Kids Events ie piano, swimming	_____
Gifts (b-day, anniversary etc.)	_____	Computer software etc	_____
Hobbies	_____	Charitable Donations	_____
Pet Costs	_____	Netflix, Hulu, Disney +, etc	_____
Travel	_____	Spotify, Apple Music etc	_____
Starbucks / Tim Horton	_____	All Other Expenses	_____
Vacations	_____	Other	_____
Lunches at work	_____	Other	_____
Cannabis products	_____	Other	_____
Fitness/Gym Memberships	_____	Other	_____
Health Care - Vitamins etc.	_____	Other	_____
Gifts (b-day, anniversary etc.)	_____	Other	
Hobbies	_____		
Pet Costs	_____		
Travel	_____		
Starbucks / Tim Horton	_____		
Vacations	_____		
Lunches at work	_____		
Cannabis products	_____		

GODFROY FINANCIAL

Essential Tax Numbers

Working Individuals

Maximum RRSP contribution: The maximum contribution for 2023 is $30,780; The 2024 limit is $31,560.

TFSA limit: In 2023, the annual limit is $6,500, for a total of $88,000 for someone who has never contributed and has been eligible for the TFSA since its introduction in 2009.

Maximum pensionable earnings: For 2023, the maximum pensionable earnings amount is $66,600 (up from $64,900 in 2022), and the basic exemption amount remains $3,500 in 2023.

Maximum EI insurable earnings: The maximum annual insurable earnings (federal) for 2023 is $61,500, up from $60,300 in 2022.

Lifetime capital gains exemption: The lifetime capital gains exemption is $971,190 in 2023, up from $913,630 in 2022.

Low-interest loans: The family loan rate until Dec. 31 is 3%.

Home buyers' amount: Did you buy a home? You may be able to claim up to $5,000 of the purchase cost, and get a non-refundable tax credit of up to $750. (*Legislation is pending* that would double the amount to $10,000 for a non-refundable tax credit of up to $1,500.)

Medical expenses threshold: For the 2023 tax year, the maximum is 3% of net income or $2,635, whichever is less.

Basic personal amount: The basic personal amount for 2023 is $15,000 for taxpayers with net income of $165,430 or less. At income levels above $165,430, the basic personal amount is gradually clawed back until it reaches $13,521 for net income of $235,675.

People that are 65+

Age amount: Individuals can claim this amount if they were aged 65 or older on Dec. 31 of the taxation year. The maximum amount they can claim in 2023 is $8,396, up from $7,898 in 2022.

OAS recovery threshold: If your net world income exceeds $86,912 in 2023 or $81,761 in 2022, you may have to repay part of or the entire OAS pension.

Lifetime ALDA dollar limit: The limit is $160,000 for both 2023 and 2022.

Individuals with children or dependents

Canada caregiver credit: If you have a dependent under the age of 18 who's physically or mentally impaired, you may be able to claim up to an additional $2,499 in 2023 in calculating certain non-refundable tax credits. For infirm dependents 18 or older, the amount for 2023 is $7,999.

Disability amount: This non-refundable credit is $9,428 in 2023, with a supplement up to $5,500 for those under 18 that is reduced if child care expenses are claimed.

Child disability benefit: The child disability benefit is a tax-free benefit of up to $3,173 in 2023 for families who care for a child under 18 with a severe and prolonged impairment in physical or mental functions.

Canada child benefit: In 2023, the maximum CCB benefit is $7,437 per child under six and up to $6,275 per child aged six through 17.

Federal tax brackets

Federal bracket thresholds will be adjusted higher in 2023 by 6.3%.

The 33.0% tax rate begins at taxable income of over $235,675, up from $221,708 in 2022.

The 29.0% tax rate begins at taxable income of over $165,430, up from $155,625 in 2022.

The 26.0% tax rate begins at taxable income of over $106,717 up from $100,392 in 2022.

The 20.5% tax rate begins at taxable income of over $53,359, up from $50,197 in 2022.

Income up to $53,359 is taxed at 15.0%.

Manufactured by Amazon.ca
Bolton, ON

33290971R00068